MIDDLE AGES

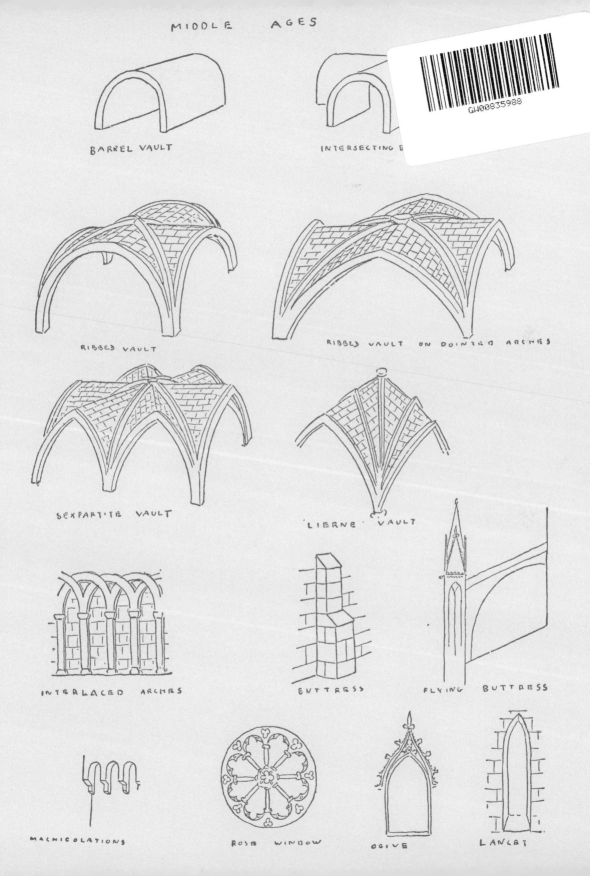

BARREL VAULT

INTERSECTING B...

RIBBED VAULT

RIBBED VAULT ON POINTED ARCHES

SEXPARTITE VAULT

LIERNE VAULT

INTERLACED ARCHES

BUTTRESS

FLYING BUTTRESS

MACHICOLATIONS

ROSE WINDOW

OGIVE

LANCET

PILLAR TO POST

PILLAR TO POST

English Architecture without Tears

BY

OSBERT LANCASTER

Illustrated by the Author

PIMPERNEL
PRESS LTD
www.pimpernelpress.com

Pimpernel Press Limited
www.pimpernelpress.com

Pillar to Post
Published as part of a set, *Osbert Lancaster's Cartoons,*
Columns and Curlicues, also including *Homes Sweet Homes*
and *Drayneflete Revealed*

First published in Great Britain 1938 by John Murray
This edition published by Pimpernel Press Limited 2015

A catalogue record for this book is available from the British Library.

ISBN 978-1-9102-5837-8

Designed by Anne Wilson
Typeset in Adobe Garamond
Printed and bound in China

10 9 8 7 6 5 4 3 2 1

To
KAREN

AUTHOR'S NOTE

All the architecture in this book is completely imaginary, and no reference is intended to any actual building living or dead.

'The art of architecture studies not structure in itself, but the effect of structure on the human spirit.'

GEOFFREY SCOTT

CONTENTS

ORDER TO VIEW

THIS is not a textbook. In the following pages the question as to whether the ogival vault first appeared at Durham or at Morienval will remain unanswered; the precise difference between Baroque and Rococo will be left undetermined; and no consideration will be given to the influence of Frank Lloyd Wright on the modern school in France. Readers who crave further enlightenment on these and kindred problems are advised to turn to some of those innumerable stout volumes that it has long been the intention of the author of the present work to read. No, this is primarily a picture book and the letterpress is intended to do no more than provide a small mass of information leavened by a large dose of personal prejudice. Nevertheless it is not entirely objectless, and even the prejudice is not without purpose, for the author is strongly of the opinion that if the present lamentable state of English architecture can be attributed to one cause rather than to another, it is due to the fact that the ordinary intelligent member of the public when confronted with architecture, whether good, bad or indifferent, remains resolutely dumb – in both the original and transatlantic senses of the word. People who can do no more than pick out the 'Merry Peasant' with one finger will not hesitate to lay down the law about music; young ladies whose acquaintance with art is confined to an unbridled enthusiasm for the works of Mr Russell Flint and a talent for depicting old world gardens on lamp shades are accustomed to give forcible expression to their views on modern painting; but persons of far greater knowledge and taste who have been living in houses, walking down streets and working in offices all their lives, are seldom so bold as to express any opinion on architecture. And however annoying the criticism of the uninstructed may be to artists and musicians, the architect cannot afford to shut his ears to the comments of the market place. An ivory tower, whether Gothic, Modernistic or Bankers' Georgian in style, is no place for him to set up his drawing board.

For of all the arts architecture is the one with which the public are most vitally concerned. A man may never enter a concert hall or a picture gallery, open a book of poems or sit through a play, but we all need shelter, and its provision, save in the case of boy scouts and troglodytes, is the business of the architect. Architecture, therefore, by reason of its twofold nature, half art, half science, is peculiarly dependent on the tastes and demands of the layman, and whereas in the other arts a neglected genius working in his garret may just conceivably produce a masterpiece, no architect has ever produced anything of lasting significance in the absence of a receptive public.

Today architecture is an activity about which the average man cares little and knows less, and such views as he may hold are founded not on any personal bias, which might be regrettable but would certainly be excusable, but on a variety of acquired misconceptions. This was not always the case; in the eighteenth century every well-educated man considered himself entitled to express his opinion about the moulding of a cornice or the disposition of a pilaster, and in nine cases out of ten was possessed of sufficient knowledge to lend it weight. But early in the nineteenth century this happy state of affairs came to an end and architecture was removed from the sphere of everyday life and placed under the jealous guardianship of experts and æsthetes. Faith became a substitute for knowledge and very soon the ordinary person came to consider architecture in the same light as higher mathematics or Hegelian philosophy; as something which he could never hope properly to understand and possessed of a scale of values that he must take on trust. With the advent of Mr Ruskin, whose distinction it was to express in prose of incomparable grandeur thought of an unparalleled confusion, this divorce from reality became complete, and in less than no time the whole theory of architecture had become hopelessly confounded with morals, religion and a great many other things with which it had not the least connection; while its practice went rapidly to pot.

However, while Mr Ruskin and his fellows were only too happy to relieve the man in the street from any further necessity to use his own judgment in the matter of architecture, they nevertheless succeeded in implanting all too firmly in his mind – not, it must be admitted, altogether intentionally – a lasting impression that what was old was automatically good, and the older, within the limits of the Christian era, the better. That Mr Ruskin in his championship of the Middle Ages could not possibly foresee the lengths to which this doctrine would be carried, must readily be admitted, but nevertheless by introducing the British public to the beauties of Giotto's campanile he must be judged as being largely responsible for a monstrous union that begot the Albert Memorial and which in time has covered the face of the land with a fearful progeny of olde Tudor tea shoppes and Jacobethan filling stations.

If therefore the reader feels that the author has occasionally been a shade too flippant in his treatment of certain of the great styles of the past, he must attribute it to a firm conviction that nothing has done more to confuse and wreck the public's response to architecture than this uncritical enthusiasm for all buildings over three hundred years old: this crazy antiquarianism that exalts an indifferent piece of vaulting or a clumsy capital to a level immeasurably above that of a Georgian balcony or a well-designed engine shed solely because they happen to have been executed in the thirteenth century. Nevertheless, let him rest assured that because one does not wax enthusiastic over the west front of Salisbury it does not mean that one is blind to the grandeur of Chartres.

Lamentable in its results as was the antiquarian heresy, it nevertheless gave rise to a further misconception that was even more disastrous. Owing to the fact that almost the only buildings of the Middle Ages that had survived were churches, castles and a few town halls, a conviction arose that it was only with buildings of a similar grandeur and importance that architecture was properly concerned; that whereas cathedrals, palaces and government offices were undertakings on which the architect might rightly employ his skill, workmen's dwellings, warehouses and factories should be left to the builder and the engineer. If, however, an architect should be lured by financial or other inducements to occupy himself with the design of such pedestrian erections, then he was perfectly justified in indulging in a little make-believe and pretending that they were something quite different. Thus all over the country one finds railway stations disguised as Norman keeps, rubber factories masquerading as Egyptian temples, greenhouses dressed up to look like the Sainte Chapelle. And this tomfoolery, although less rampant than it was in the last century, is still flourishing today, and until we rid ourselves of such snobbery and realize that the cathedral, the Dean's house in the Close and the public convenience in the market square are all 'architecture', or rather all provide opportunities of varying scope and totally distinct character for the practice of architecture, there is no hope of improvement.

The object of this book, therefore, in so far as it has one, is to induce an attitude towards architecture less reverent and of greater awareness, and to encourage the reader, when driving down the bypass or riding on the tops of 'buses or just walking along the street, to take another look at the fantastic collection of buildings on either side which hitherto, maybe, he has been accustomed to accept without question on the grounds that 'that's architecture that was', and therefore not a matter on which he could possibly be expected to hold any views.

If this seems a burden at once too pompous and too heavy for so slight a volume, the author must gracefully relinquish it, once more remarking that this is, after all, just a picture book.

O.L.

EGYPT

THE architecture of ancient Egypt has much to commend it – size, dignity and durability – but nevertheless it must be admitted that it is a trifle monotonous. As a monument the pyramid is undoubtedly impressive, but economically difficult to justify, and in the other more mundane forms of Egyptian architecture the same complete disregard of expenditure, of time, of labour and of space is, though less splendidly evident, always discernible. Very early in the world's history the Egyptian architects realized that the simplest method of covering any enclosed space with a roof was to place beams across from wall to wall, supported where necessary by pillars. The size of the space thus covered was only limited by the size of the single unbroken slabs of stone readily obtainable. As the Nile valley was well supplied with suitable quarries, and an enormous amount of slave labour was always at hand to raise these monoliths by physical exertion, the resulting temples were exceedingly lofty, and doubtless their builders were completely satisfied. But the very ease with which such tremendous buildings could be erected led inevitably to a species of architectural atrophy. This one problem being solved so soon, no further inventiveness was called for, as no further demands were ever made on the ingenuity of the Egyptian architect. Century after century exactly the same type of buildings were erected; in times of plenty the workmanship was finer and the decoration a little richer than usual, and in times of trouble the details tended to be scamped; these seem, to all but archæologists, the only visible differences over a period of nearly three thousand years.

The interior decoration and furniture of these buildings has unfortunately been preserved all too well in the tombs of the Pharaohs and when from time to time fresh examples appear, which, without the excavators' word for their authenticity, one might well be pardoned for supposing to have been purchased at the sale of effects of some Second Empire *cocotte* kept by a Jewish impresario of antiquarian tastes, they are greeted with the greatest enthusiasm and no time is lost in applying the more striking and offensive motifs to the decoration of super-cinemas and factories on the bypass.

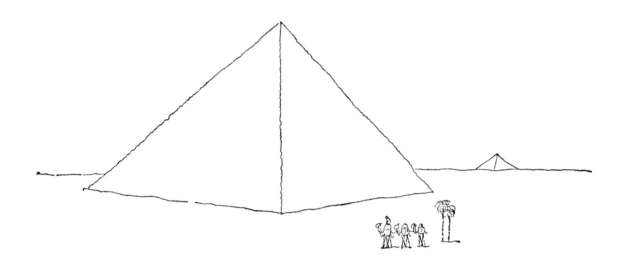

'THERE was no passion in this architecture,' remarks a modern traveller, recording his impressions of the Parthenon, 'it was like a complicated and varying formula in three dimensions that is so very easy when you know how.' Which sums up very neatly the three great characteristics of the first of the world's great architectural styles: its apparent simplicity, its actual complexity and the rigidly intellectual basis on which it rests. It was a method of building in wood that had been adapted, and successfully adapted, to construction in stone, which renders it incidentally a most useful stick with which to beat the modern devotees of truthful construction at all costs. The basis of the style was the lintel, that is to say, the horizontal wooden beam resting on two or more uprights, but on this simple foundation has been raised the subtlest, the most complete and the most purely logical style of architecture that the world has ever known.

It is customary to speak of the three 'orders' of Greek architecture – the Doric, the Ionic and the Corinthian – each of which while differing in such details as the moulding of the cornice, the decoration of the entablature and the form of capitals of the columns, embodies the same constructional principles, but in actual fact it was the first and greatest of these, the Doric, that was employed almost exclusively during the great period of Greek civilization and which really merits the name of Greek architecture.

At first sight it seems that nothing could be easier than the correct marshalling of these rows of simple columns and it is only when one understands how large a part illusion plays, how many of these seemingly straight lines are actually curved, that one realizes what a miraculous sense of proportion, how formidable a knowledge of mathematics and what centuries of practice and experiment have been involved in the achievement of this final impression of inspired simplicity.

Incidentally, a slight acquaintance with this cunning trickery that makes the curved appear straight and the straight curved is extremely useful on a Hellenic cruise, where much money may then be won by casual wagers with rural Deans.

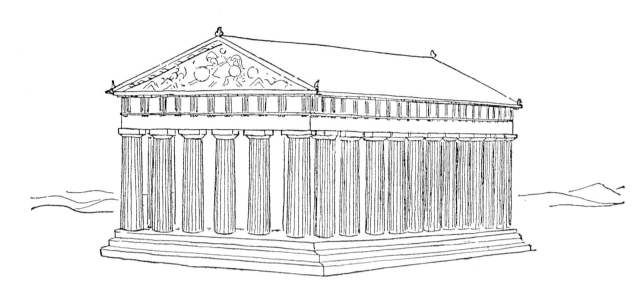

THE taste of the Romans, like that of so many Empire builders, tended towards the flamboyant, and it was not surprising therefore that they should have had the temerity to try to improve on the architecture of the Greeks. That this attempt was crowned with but indifferent success is still less remarkable, in that the Greeks had brought their particular type of building to so complete a state of perfection that no further development along those particular lines was possible. However, the Romans introduced several remarkable innovations, of which the most daring was the adaptation of the Orders to the construction of buildings of two storeys, by superimposing one row of columns on the top of another; a constructional device that was to provide the basis of much of the architecture of the Renaissance. Another device for the popularization, if not the discovery, of which the Romans were responsible was the round arch, which they used in conjunction with the column to form an arcade.

It is not surprising that it should have been the Corinthian, the last and flashiest of the three Greek orders, which the Romans used most frequently, nor that in their efforts to outdo the Greeks they should have been led to concentrate on an extreme richness of decoration, which must, one imagines, have rendered Rome in all its glory a trifle overpowering. Augustus, we are told, found the city brick and left it marble, but several of the recent changes in London do not encourage one to believe that such a metamorphosis is necessarily a change for the better.

However, when the Romans forgot for a moment to outdo the Greeks and busied themselves with works such as aqueducts, roads and fortifications, which we should consider to belong to the province of the engineer, they revealed their real genius for construction, and produced monuments that entitle their architecture to a consideration no less serious than that universally accorded to the Greek.

THERE was one feat of construction that the Romans with all their engineering ability had never been able, any more than the Greeks, to achieve. They were perfectly capable of putting a dome on a circular building, but the difficulty of covering a rectangular edifice with this type of roof had always defeated them. The final solution of this problem was reserved for the architects of Byzantium; that is, the satisfactory solution, for a method of raising a dome on squinches (reducing the square to be covered to an approximate circle by placing beams across the corners) had been practised in the East for centuries; but the development of the true dome, one resting on pendentives, was Byzantium's great contribution to Western architecture. In the case of England it was a gift which was not applied until centuries later, and by the time that St Paul's had arisen the dome had been developed and exploited by several generations of Italian and French architects. Nevertheless the credit belongs in the first instance to the Byzantines.

Apart from this one very indirect contribution, and although Santa Sophia ranks with St Peter's and Chartres as one of the three great masterpieces of Christian art, Byzantine architecture has exercised no influence on that of England, and until Westminster Cathedral was built no architect had had the courage to attempt to revive it.

The figure in the foreground on the opposite page is Mr Robert Byron, heavily disguised.

THE earliest mode of building employed in England was one in which everything, including shelter, was sacrificed to obtain an effect of rugged grandeur. Simple in design, the principal buildings in this style nevertheless presented a series of exceedingly tricky problems of construction, and the labour and ingenuity required to manœuvre the vast monoliths into position must have been considerable. The successful achievement of such feats (without the assistance of any cranes and machinery) indicates the existence, even in that remote age, of that spirit of dogged perseverance and tenacity which has done so much to make British architecture what it is today. Incidentally it is interesting to note that even then British architects were actuated by a profound faith, which has never subsequently wavered, in the doctrine that the best architecture is that which involves the most trouble.

The actual date of such erections as that represented on the opposite page has never been accurately determined; the building in the left foreground, however, can with some degree of confidence be assigned to the second or third decade of the twentieth century AD.

NORMAN

THE earliest style of medieval architecture in Western Europe is known as Romanesque, save in England, where, for patriotic reasons, it is always referred to as Norman. It was an admirable, straightforward method of building – what the French call 'une architecture franche' – with none of those sleight-of-hand tricks that for some people render the later Gothic styles so disturbing, and flourished until the close of the twelfth century. The enormous pillars quite obviously support the roof and together with the immensely thick walls give the spectator a welcome feeling of security. One never receives the impression that a Norman church has by some curious natural process sprung up out of the ground; the first glance is sufficient to assure one that its construction has cost a great many people a great deal of very hard work. Owing to the simplicity of their construction almost all the examples of this style achieve a dignity and a repose which is frequently lacking in later buildings whose more complicated and scientific structural methods have presented the builders with greater opportunities for exercising their imagination.

For the amateur the Norman style possesses another great advantage; of all the medieval styles it is far the easiest to recognize. Once you have assured yourself that the arches are round not pointed, you are in a position to pronounce with conviction that it is a Norman building at which you are looking. And in nine cases out of ten you will be right, for luckily Mr Ruskin and the other nineteenth-century revivalists did not consider Norman a sufficiently fancy style to merit revival for ecclesiastical purposes, and in modern times it has been confined almost exclusively to railway tunnels. In Germany, however, where of course it was known as Romanesque, it was regarded more favourably, and several very fine barracks and even one or two churches were built in this style.

LATE in the late twelfth century some anonymous genius discovered a new method of vaulting whereby the masonry of the roof was supported by a series of stone ribs, and the whole body of architects, fired by the spirit of competition, set to and in very short time evolved a number of ingenious improvements. Hitherto, a very large number of pillars and immensely thick walls had been necessary, but now it was discovered that by means of a judicious disposition of buttresses and the new system of vaulting used in conjunction with the pointed arch, the weight could be more evenly distributed and a greater proportion of wall-space devoted to windows. Although it is sometimes maintained that the credit for this revolutionary discovery belongs to an anonymous Englishman, it cannot be denied that the French made far better use of it and that the Early English style produced no single building in any way comparable with Chartres. At the same time there developed an enormous enthusiasm for decoration which found its chief outlet in covering the capitals of the pillars, the surrounds of the doors and windows and in fact every available space with a riot of intricate carving, producing an effect which (in the case of most of the English examples) it must be confessed was ingenious rather than beautiful.

Another notable feature of the style were the west fronts of the cathedrals and larger churches, which were covered from top to bottom with sculptured figures arranged in rows of niches, representing the most notable figures of the Old and New Testaments and a large selection of saints. It is customary to refer to these façades as the poor man's Bible – a custom which prompts the reflection that the poor man of the Middle Ages must have enjoyed quite exceptional eyesight. In the hands of a master, as at Peterborough, the effect can be overwhelmingly beautiful, but it was a device that needed very careful handling and none but the most pig-headed medievalist can sincerely maintain that in the west front of Salisbury for instance, the thirteenth century yields anything to our own in the way of pointless confusion and downright ugliness.

DECORATED

AT the beginning of the fourteenth century Gothic building underwent a further change, and the resulting style is frequently known as Decorated (for reasons that remain a trifle obscure in that, in most cases, the decoration, though invariably rich, is not noticeably more conspicuous than in either of the other two styles of Gothic architecture). The most notable development which distinguished this new style from Early English was in the windows. Formerly these had been of narrow lancet shape, and when a large window was required at the east end or at the termination of the transepts, this could only be obtained by grouping three lancets together with the tallest in the centre. With improved methods of construction it was now found possible to build thinner walls, and so the divisions between the lancets were reduced to two thin shafts terminating in elaborate tracery of curvilinear design. Alongside this elaboration in the treatment of the windows there occurred a corresponding development in the construction of the pillars. Already in Early English churches the pillar had been enriched by the addition of subsidiary shafts tacked on to the sides supporting the vaulting; now it vanishes completely and its place is taken by a sheaf of slender columns of equal size.

Of the three styles of Gothic architecture in England it is the Decorated that has been the most frequently undervalued. The virtuosity and breathtaking qualities of Perpendicular and Ruskin's powerful championship of the simple virtues of Early English have both tended to overshadow its less obvious beauties. Moreover, with the exception of Exeter it is not a style that is worthily represented in our cathedrals. But nevertheless, some may consider it the greatest of the three, for in the finest examples (the parish churches of East Anglia, for instance) there is evidence of a mastery over materials to which the Early English architects never attained and which the Perpendicular architects frequently abused.

UNLIKE the other three styles of medieval architecture, which were common to all northern Europe, Perpendicular was a purely English discovery and its masterpieces cannot be paralleled anywhere abroad. This style, which attained to its fullest development in the second half of the fifteenth century, was the logical outcome of a curious passion for height, operating within the conventions of the Decorated style of the previous age. All the elements of the latter style are still here but curiously distorted and changed; the vertical lines have become fantastically prolonged and when at last they curve inwards they do so far more abruptly, giving to the resulting arch a curiously flattened form. In addition, a number of horizontal bars appear in the tracery of the windows, rendered essential by the need to provide some support for the thin perpendicular shafts. At the same time the system of vaulting grew ever more complex and it became customary to indulge in a superabundance of ribs and bosses, the majority of which fulfilled no structural purpose, until finally the system known as 'fan vaulting' was evolved; an architectural device which arouses enormous enthusiasm on account of the difficulties it has all too obviously involved but which from an aesthetic standpoint frequently belongs to the 'Last-Supper-carved-on-a-peachstone' class of masterpiece. Externally the most remarkable features of the style were the flying buttresses, which although they occur in other methods of building, are here developed to a most fantastic pitch of ingenuity. It is as though the Perpendicular architect abhorred any unnecessary expanse of masonry and was desirous of eliminating every square inch of solid stone that was not absolutely essential to the stability of the building; even battlements which were still retained round the roof for decorative purposes were pierced and hollowed until they resembled nothing so much as a plan or map of themselves. Many of the most notable examples of the style differ from vast conservatories only in that the framework is of stone, not iron or wood and that the glass is coloured.

Nevertheless, with all its grandeur and beauty it must be admitted that Perpendicular remains, in most cases, an essentially virtuoso performance compelling an admiration that is not far removed from astonishment.

TUDOR

DURING the Middle Ages the science of architecture had seldom been applied to domestic building save in the most rudimentary fashion. It was the Church which had cultivated and developed architecture, as it had the other arts, and applied it to the erection of cathedrals, churches and monasteries. Of the laity far the largest class, the agricultural labourers, lived in primitive cottages built of mud (as they still were in certain parts of the country, notably Devonshire, until quite recently); the burghers, although latterly often in a position to spend time and money on the decoration of their houses, were prevented by the cramped conditions of the walled town from indulging in any elaborate architectural experiments; the nobility, up to the very end of the period, were only interested in those aspects of the science which dealt with fortification. Even so vast and celebrated a building as the royal palace of Clarendon seems to have been little but an enormous collection of halls and small rooms, all on one level, added to and enlarged as convenience and the whims of various monarchs dictated, enclosed by a moat and wall, and presenting hardly any features of strictly architectural interest.

But with the firm establishment of the Tudors conditions altered and the country gentry had now the leisure and the necessary assurance of safety to turn their minds to the development of the unfortified manor house. The actual appearance of such houses differed widely from district to district; in some parts the presence of quarries near at hand enabled the builder to work in stone, elsewhere he was forced to be content with timber and plaster or in certain districts brick. The actual form of the house was dictated by the material, but the plan in every case remained in its essentials medieval, for although the country no longer suffered from constant civil wars the memories of past dangers were still vivid and led to the retention of many of the features of the castle.

ELIZABETHAN

THE parallel between the age of Queen Victoria and that of Queen Elizabeth has provoked frequent comment and explanation. Both, it is frequently pointed out, were ages of expansion and both made imperishable contributions to our national literature. What, however, is rather less often commented on is that both were periods in which the fine arts achieved a new low. For as far as architecture and decoration are concerned the background against which Shakespeare lived and worked was hardly more attractive than that which displayed Alfred Lord Tennyson to such advantage.

In the arts the age of Elizabeth was one of transition; the old medieval restraints had been abandoned, but nothing as yet had appeared to take their place, so that the architects with a number of new processes at their disposal were at a complete loss as how best to apply them. As a result houses increased enormously in size but not in beauty. The comparative cheapness of glass led to a sudden enlargement of the windows, that had hitherto been extremely small, producing an effect that called forth the comment that such houses were 'more glass than wall'. Vague rumours of what was happening in Italy together with a sudden flood of cheap and ill-drawn pattern books containing what the artists hoped were classical details encouraged architects to embellish the gaunt and still fortress-like mansions of the nobility with a fiendish variety of pilasters and cornices of the proper meaning and application of which they were totally unaware. The tremendous literary enthusiasm of the period invaded architecture and led to the introduction of numerous mottoes as decorative features which appeared in every available position, both inside and out.

In certain districts, notably Gloucestershire, a pleasant and unpretentious style of domestic architecture was evolved which so long as it remained unaffected by foreign influences produced buildings of much merit and charm. Needless to say when, late in the nineteenth century, an Elizabethan revival took place, it was the flashiest and most grandiose specimens that were taken as models.

RENAISSANCE

WHILE in England men were busy raising those fantastic ecclesiastical conservatories in the perpendicular style of Gothic architecture, in Italy architects were already busily engaged on the first and greatest of revivals. Why the ruins of ancient Rome, which had been visible for centuries, should suddenly have attracted attention at this particular moment in time is a question to which the reader will find no answer here. However, whatever the reason may have been, it was a highly welcome development, for the Gothic style was finished; after the Perpendicular, and kindred styles abroad, no further development was possible and the latest examples exhibit many of the signs of complete spiritual exhaustion.

In classifying Renaissance architecture as a revival one is perhaps guilty of a misstatement, for while Greece and Rome supplied both the inspiration and the architectural motifs of the style, and although Renaissance architects all paid homage to Vitruvius and boasted of the accuracy with which they followed his precepts, in practice they never hesitated to abandon them whenever their fancy dictated, and thus their buildings may be said to represent a development and an extension of the classic tradition rather than a slavish resuscitation of a long lost method of building. For a long time England had little or no share in this new movement, and until the seventeenth century the only signs that a fundamental change had taken place in architectural theory and practice were a few inexpertly copied capitals and pilasters tacked on to the fabric of houses which remained resolutely medieval in plan and construction. Although long delayed, the English Renaissance was destined to have a truly splendid flowering, and in Inigo Jones and Sir Christopher Wren it produced two architects who need not fear comparison with any of the great masters. In fact, this time lag may be said to have been an advantage, for when English architects first became acquainted with Italian architecture, it was already an established style with many different schools and variations, and they could view it with a thoroughness and a detachment that would have been impossible at the time of its enthusiastic inception.

THE first Renaissance style to be introduced into England was the Palladian, so-called after Palladio who had developed it in north Italy in the sixteenth century, and Inigo Jones was its principal, in fact almost its only, exponent. (One of the results of the Renaissance had been the appearance of the individual architect; in the Middle Ages architecture had been largely a corporative activity, and its practitioners have remained in almost every case anonymous.) But in the second half of the seventeenth century there emerged the figure of the second of our great English architects, and one of the greatest architects of all time, Sir Christopher Wren, who although he had no first-hand acquaintance with the architecture of Italy, evolved from it a style less rigid than the Palladian, of a greater richness and one that was completely suited to the English climate and character.

The greatest achievements of this style were St Paul's Cathedral, and the innumerable city churches built by Wren and his pupils after the Great Fire. Here one is at a loss to know what to admire most; the seemingly endless variety of treatment and invention which achieves the miracle of avoiding all suspicion of sameness and monotony in half a hundred different churches all erected within a few years of each other; the restraint of the handling coupled with the largeness of the conception which prevents grandeur from declining into the merely grandiose; or the incredible skill and ingenuity with which so, at first sight, intractably Gothic a feature as the church spire (a form which the English medieval builder had developed with conspicuous success and one which therefore possessed a national significance) was preserved and reinterpreted in classical terms, although quite unknown to antiquity.

In one respect only did the builders of these masterpieces fail; they not infrequently chose sites which the churchmen of a later age considered might be sold for much money and given, if not to the poor, at least to the Ecclesiastical Commissioners.

GEO. REX FID DEF MDCCXX

ON THIS SITE WILL
BE ERECTED THE
MAGNIFICENT
NEW PREMISES
OF THE
PROSCENE
DEVELOPMENT Co

BAROQUE

THE characteristic that distinguished the Renaissance from all other revivalist movements, both architectural and religious, was its almost inexhaustible vitality. After the first rush of enthusiasm it did not peter out and die; the vital creative force behind it continued to function for close on four hundred years, constantly discovering new forms of expression while still employing the same classical idiom. It was as though an ingenious small boy was bent on discovering how many different buildings he could put up with the same box of bricks. Halfway through the seventeenth century, however, it appeared as though every possible combination had been exhausted, whereupon the small boy, not in the least deterred, proceeded to use his bricks as counters in a dazzling display of juggling.

This ability to employ architectural forms for purposes which they had never been intended – in order to express movement or obtain an effect of drama – and get away with it, was the whole secret of Baroque. Vast flights of steps, innumerable statues, elaborate fountains were all pressed into service for the sake of a truly impressive effect, to obtain which the Baroque architect did not hesitate to twist columns until they looked like sticks of barley sugar, cover cornices in rich folds of imitation drapery, extend façades until they were twice the height of the buildings they masked, and finally if time or money ran out to paint whole vistas of staircases and colonnades he was unable to achieve three-dimensionally. That it was a highly dangerous proceeding, that could be justified only by complete success and called for an almost incredible degree of virtuosity on the part of the architect, was proved by the unhappy efforts to revive it made in England at the beginning of the present century (see Edwardian Baroque).

It is not therefore surprising that with the solitary exception of Vanbrugh, no English architect of that period was encouraged to try his hand at the Baroque, for cleverness is a quality that, in architecture no less than in life, we have always been notorious for regarding with ill-concealed dislike.

QUEEN ANNE

THE style of domestic architecture illustrated on the opposite page is frequently referred to as Queen Anne, although few monarchs have displayed less interest in architecture than that sovereign; nor was its practice confined to her reign. It would be both more rational and more just to call it Wren, for it was first brought to a state of perfection by that great man and further developed and popularized by his immediate followers. It was the first fully developed style of domestic architecture to be employed in England. Here the cornice, pilaster and other motifs borrowed at second hand from classical antiquity have become completely assimilated and, used in conjunction with brick, form the foundation of a great national tradition.

Although it is customary to regard the numerous country houses and palaces as the great masterpieces of the style, Wren and his followers may perhaps be considered even more worthy of praise for their triumphs in urban architecture, for it was their peculiar merit to have devised, at a time when the whole capital had to be rebuilt after the Great Fire, a type of house that was not only completely satisfactory in itself, but one which could always be employed as a unit in a larger scheme. They did their duty not only by the householder but also by the street. And the fact that their example was followed by all the various schools of architecture that flourished throughout the eighteenth century, and was only neglected in the nineteenth, is responsible for much of whatever architectural merit London as a city may still be thought to possess.

GEORGIAN (TOWN)

THE expansion of London and the increase, both in numbers and importance, of the middle class, provided the eighteenth-century architect with one of his most important tasks. The problem of housing large numbers of city merchants and professional men, all with big families, at no great distance from their place of business, at the same time maintaining some order and dignity in the process of extending the city, was not a light one, but nevertheless the solution arrived at was, granted the social conditions of the time, as nearly perfect as possible and constitutes one of the great triumphs of English architecture. This happy result was largely brought about by the development in combination of the two great discoveries of contemporary town planning – the terrace and the square. The first presented the architect with a unit sufficiently large to allow him to achieve impressive and dignified effects, which his descendant who is forced to manipulate a row of detached houses designed for clients clamouring for something different, in a pathetic effort to assert an individuality they do not, in fact, possess, can never hope to emulate today. The second preserved sufficient of the country in the shape of grass and trees to form an agreeable contrast with the surrounding bricks and mortar and sufficient light, air and space to render it pleasant and healthy and to facilitate the movement of traffic.

Today we are busy pulling down these districts as quickly as possible on the grounds that the houses are difficult to run, which may be true, and sneering at them on the grounds that they are monotonous, which certainly is not. By means of such simple devices as the depressed arch, the decorated fanlight and the sculptured keystone, the eighteenth-century architect avoided monotony with a skill and a subtlety which seems always to elude the designers of the pseudo-American cliff-dwellings of Park Lane. For the boredom occasioned by too much restraint is always preferable to that produced by an uncontrolled enthusiasm for a pointless variety.

GEORGIAN (COUNTRY)

I N the second quarter of the eighteenth century there arose among English intellectuals an extreme enthusiasm for Italy and things Italian, and a young man's education was considered incomplete if he had not visited that country. Very soon in all the arts, but more particularly music and architecture, it became de rigueur slavishly to copy Italian models. As a result the popularity of the Palladian style, that had first been introduced nearly a century earlier by Inigo Jones, enjoyed a new lease of life, and one enthusiastic and noble amateur even went so far as to erect on the banks of the Thames a house that was a model of a villa that Palladio had built on the banks of the Brenta.

At first sight it might be thought that this new Palladian revival would have had a stultifying and unhealthy effect on English architecture, but happily such was not the case, for the English architect, if sometimes a little lacking in originality, has always displayed a remarkable skill at adaptation (unfortunately he has not always been endowed with a correspondingly developed ability to exercise his judgment in respect to the models he adapts), and it was not long before the style had become completely acclimatized.

About the middle of the century it was further modified by a renewed interest in antiquity, which led to a further adaptation, this time, however, at first hand, of motifs from Greek architecture. It might be thought that a style to the formation of which so many diverse elements had gone – Palladian, Wren, Palladian again, Greek Revival – and which paid such attention to various academic formulae, would have been unlikely to produce many masterpieces. Whereas, in fact, whatever buildings may be thought to entitle English architecture to a place alongside that of the other countries of Western Europe, were almost all produced in the period which started after the Great Fire and ended on the death of George III. Which just shows that in architecture it is the architect, not the formula, which counts.

GOTHICK

OWARDS the end of the eighteenth century there was noticeable in almost every sphere of human activity a growing craving for Romance. In architecture this nostalgia was particularly marked and took the form of a polite enthusiasm for the styles of far away and long ago. Chinese, Indian, Egyptian and Gothic methods of building all in turn enjoyed a remarkable vogue among the cognoscenti, but it was the last style that proved most popular and the revival of which was to prove, though not at once, most disastrous for English architecture. So long as the traditions and conventions governing the thought and manners of the eighteenth century remained in force, all was well. The patrons of architecture were enlightened and well-educated men who were perfectly aware that a wholesale revival of Gothic methods of building would be intolerable, but regarded, quite rightly, the building of a cottage or two in what they hoped was a medieval but were quite certain was a picturesque style, as perfectly permissible. Thus the gazebos, the *cottages ornés* and the summer houses which formed the principal output of the Gothic architects of the period, bore little relation to any known Gothic style; they remained, in fact, perfectly ordinary eighteenth-century cottages on to which had been tacked a row of castellations and a couple of plaster gargoyles. Ninety per cent of these productions had little connection with architecture at all but were simply the work of smart interior decorators trying their hand at landscape gardening, or literary amateurs of exhibitionist tendencies creating a suitable background for their carefully cultivated personalities. Nevertheless, out of this innocuous and rather charming chrysalis would one day come blundering the dreary great moth of Victorian revivalism.

REGENCY

T the beginning of the nineteenth century the rapid rate of London's expansion was still further accelerated, and it was the great merit of the architects of the day, of whom the most memorable though not the most gifted was Nash, that they realized that if chaos was to be averted, all future developments must be considered not as isolated streets and districts but as part of one rational and carefully considered plan. If the numerous new squares and crescents that were then put up all over London, but more particularly in the north-west, were not the equal of the best work of the previous generation, it was largely the result of the speed with which they were erected, which led to the sacrifice of detail for the sake of a fine general effect. It is this preoccupation with the total mass that gives to the best Regency architecture its impressive vistas and slight but not unwelcome theatrical air.

But while the greatest triumphs of the style were gained in the design and layout of large terraces, it proved almost equally successful when applied on a smaller scale. The numerous villas erected at this time both in London and along the coast – incidentally no one has ever devised a style of building that harmonized better with the scenery and atmosphere of the English seaside – with their delicate ironwork balconies, their ingenious and successful bow windows, and their coats of sensible and attractive stucco, are among the most charming and original small buildings in the whole history of English architecture.

'IN these years' (1850–70), as Mr Guedalla informs us, 'a noble impulse among architects was covering England with reproductions of the medieval antique, of which the Law Courts are the stateliest, the Randolph Hotel at Oxford not the least worthy example.' By the middle of the nineteenth century the Gothic Revival had ceased to be a joke; the driving force behind it had changed from fashionable whimsy to an evangelical (the word is used in no narrow denominational sense) fervour. The Gothic was now regarded not merely as the most beautiful method of building but also the most True; a practical demonstration of the permanent validity of Keats' celebrated definition of æsthetic worth. It was a shrewd move on the part of the poet to inform us, albeit rather tartly, that the interchangeability of Truth and Beauty 'is all we need to know', for despite the gallant efforts of Mr Ruskin, embodied in a score of thick volumes, the precise reason why any one style of building should be Truer than another remains impenetrably obscure.

The revivalists, however, were not burdened with overmuch intellectual curiosity, and taking the poet at his word forged ahead, creating for posterity a noble legacy of schools, town halls and railway termini all in the purest style of the thirteenth and fourteenth centuries. At first they had confined themselves largely to ecclesiastical buildings, but had soon come to the conclusion that what was good enough for God was good enough for Caesar and in less than no time half the public buildings in the country were enriched by a splendid abundance of crockets and gargoyles, *meurtrières* and encaustic tiling.

To a lay observer it might seem that one of the principal objections to the revival of the Gothic style lay in the fact that it had evolved under conditions which found no parallel in the modern world, but in practice this objection was found to be invalid. Indeed, its greatest merit in the eyes of the architect of the period lay in its splendid adaptability, and when Sir Gilbert Scott's plan for a Gothic Foreign Office had to be abandoned owing to the unenlightened attitude of Lord Palmerston, he was able by a few strokes of the pen to transform it into St Pancras Railway Station.

WHILE the more ambitious nineteenth-century manifestations of the Gothic spirit in architecture may, with very few exceptions, be dismissed as deplorable, certain of the minor achievements still retain a vague period charm. In particular some of the smaller country railway stations represent a most unexpectedly successful outcome of a brave, but admittedly uncalled for, attempt to adapt the methods of building popular in ecclesiastical circles in the fourteenth century to the needs of the machine age. Their merits, it must be admitted, have very little connection with architecture, but nevertheless they frequently achieve an air of cosy whimsicality not out of keeping with the spirit of our British Railways. Moreover, it cannot be denied that up till the present none of the Railway Companies (with the honourable exception of London Transport) have evolved a style for this particular type of building that is not equally inconvenient and twice as offensive.

Another branch of architecture in which this unpretentious form of Gothicism operated, with, alas, considerably less success, was the erection of public conveniences. These necessary and useful reminders of the limitations of humanity present a difficult problem for the architect; no one wishes that they shall be overwhelmingly conspicuous, but on the other hand they would belie their name were they too cunningly concealed.

The Gothic revivalists' gallant attempt to combine modesty with prominence by erecting small-scale models of fourteenth-century baptisteries in cast iron and equipping them with the necessary plumbing was not, however, a solution to the problem that entitles them to any praise save on the score of ingenuity.

KENSINGTON ITALIANATE

ALTHOUGH the Gothic revival was making rapid headway throughout the early years of Queen Victoria's reign it did not attain to its greatest popularity until the 'sixties and 'seventies, and while an ever-increasing number of churches and town halls were erected in that style, domestic architecture remained for a long time unaffected. Thus when the great expansion of London during the 'forties and 'fifties led to the development of Belgravia, Paddington and Kensington, the terraces and squares which were erected in these districts were built in a style which, despite a certain monotony and, according to modern standards, considerable inconvenience, did nevertheless represent the last expiring flicker of the great classic tradition of English architecture. Although the detail was usually inferior to that of the best Regency work and the remarkable inventiveness of that style was lacking, Kensington Italianate at its best, e.g. Belgrave Square, did achieve dignity and even a certain magnificence. And even when, as has happened in North Kensington and elsewhere, whole streets and terraces intended for prosperous stockbrokers have sunk to the slum level, they still retain some faint atmosphere of shabby grandeur. (The ability to survive drastic social reverses forms an acid test for architecture and one which it can be confidently said that the arterial housing estates, the slums of the future, will certainly not be capable of satisfying.)

However, despite the impressive effect of the façades, houses built in the Kensington Italianate possessed numerous defects, such as airless and pitch-dark basements and far too many and too steep stairs. In addition, in order to create the full architectural effect intended by the builder it is necessary that all the houses in a block or terrace should receive a coat of stucco of the same colour and at the same time; a condition which the sturdy individualism of the average British householder has always rendered impossible of fulfilment. Nevertheless, their total disappearance, which seems to be merely a matter of time, will deprive London of much of its character, which the luxury flats and cosy little maisonnettes in Architectural Association Georgian, which are already taking their place in Paddington, will do nothing to restore.

SALUBRIOUS DWELLINGS FOR THE INDUSTRIOUS ARTISAN

On earth the God of Wealth was made
Sole patron of the building Trade.

Swift

WHILE the Victorian architects were busy erecting tasteful reproductions of Chartres cathedral and the belfry of Bruges (so useful for factory chimneys) and covering the rather inefficiently drained marshes on the outskirts of Westminster with the stucco palaces of the nobility and gentry, it must not be imagined that the needs of the humbler classes of the community were in any way overlooked. In all the great new towns of the Midlands and the Industrial North large housing estates sprang up on which, by the exercise of remarkable forethought and ingenuity, so great was the anxiety lest the worker should be too far removed from the sights and sounds of the factory or mine which was the scene of his cheerful labour, a quite fantastic number of working families were accommodated. In order that the inhabitants might have the privilege of contemplating, almost ceaselessly, the visible tokens of nineteenth-century man's final triumph over nature, many of these estates were carefully built alongside the permanent way, or even, if there was a viaduct handy, actually underneath it. That the humble householders might recall the country villages from which so many of them had come, the streets were considerately left unpaved and the drainage system was made to conform to the primitive rustic models to which they were accustomed. It is true that it was found impossible to avoid a certain monotony but this was counteracted by carefully refraining from doing anything to interfere with the effects of the elements, and allowing the weather full opportunity to produce a fascinating variety of surface texture.

These working-class residential districts met with the complete approbation of landlords and employers alike and it was only at the very end of the century that the voices of certain muddle-headed philanthropists were heard declaring that such houses and streets were unfit for human habitation. The best answer to such officious and inexperienced busybodies is provided by the fact that today, after a lapse of nearly a century, a large portion of the population still live in them.

I N the earlier part of the nineteenth century it was assumed, and rightly, that a little healthy vulgarity and full-blooded ostentation were not out of place in the architecture and decoration of a public house, and it was during this period that the tradition governing the appearance of the English pub was evolved. While the main body of the building conformed to the rules governing South Kensington Italian, it was always enlivened by the addition of a number of decorative adjuncts which, though similar in general form, displayed an endless and fascinating variety of treatment. Of these the most important was the plate glass window, which took up a large section of the façade, and was invariably made the excuse for a virtuoso display of decorative engraving in which may frequently be detected the ingenuous working of native taste for the baroque that nowadays can only find expression in the decoration of merry-go-rounds and cigar boxes. Hardly less important were the enormous lantern which was suspended from an equally imposing and lavishly decorated curlicue at the corner of the building, the whole forming a triumph of nineteenth-century ironwork, and the splendid and elaborate examples of the signwriter's art with which the façade was always generously enlivened.

But, alas, with the spread of popular education even the brewers became cultured and the typical pub, such as the one illustrated here, gave way to every variety of Gothic hostelry and its homely façade was soon hidden behind a copious enrichment of coloured brickwork and encaustic tiles. Says Ruskin sadly, writing in 1872, 'there is scarcely a public house near the Crystal Palace but sells its gin-and-bitters under pseudo-Venetian capitals copied from the church of the Madonna of Health or of Miracles.'

But worse was still to come. Half-baked culture was succeeded by a poisonous refinement which found expression in olde worlde half-timbering and a general atmosphere of cottagey cheeriness. Fortunately a number of the old-fashioned pubs still survive in the less fashionable quarters, but the majority of them are doubtless doomed and will shortly be replaced by tasteful erections in the Bypass Elizabethan or Brewers' Georgian styles.

'WHATEVER may be said in favour of the Victorians,' remarks Mr P.G. Wodehouse, 'it is pretty generally admitted that few of them were to be trusted within reach of a trowel and a pile of bricks.' The sage when he made this profound observation was thinking of the English country house of the period; had he been referring to a similar building of the same date north of the Border it is probable that he would have expressed himself even more forcibly. For awe-inspiring as were the results of the archæological enthusiasm and light-hearted fantasy of Victorian architects working in England, these worthies seem frequently to have reserved the most ambitious efforts of their breathtaking virtuosity for the benefit of their Scottish patrons.

In a praiseworthy attempt to provide the Northern kingdom with an ample supply of stately homes, they evolved a style which they hoped adequately symbolized the rugged virtues and lurking romance of the inhabitants of

> Caledonia stern and wild,
> Meet nurse for a poetic child

and which they christened Scottish Baronial. It was, as the name implies, essentially an upper-class style and one which mirrored faithfully that passion on the part of the nobility and gentry for combining the minimum of comfort with the maximum of expense that has always exercised so great an influence over our domestic architecture. Spiral staircases of a steepness and gloom that rendered oubliettes unnecessary; small windows which made up for the amount of light they kept out by the amount of wind they let in; drains which conformed to medieval standards with an accuracy which in the rest of the structure remained an eagerly desired but as yet unattained ideal. These were among the invariable features of the style, but were looked on as but a small price to pay for the impressive silhouette, the battlements, the corbels and cloud-piercing turrets of the granite-laden exterior. Moreover, if the Dear Queen could not only endure but actually welcome these little inconveniences inseparable from a truly baronial existence in the Highlands, how could lesser mortals complain if they cracked their skulls on the old-world groining in the Baron's privy or caught pneumonia from the bracing wind that whistled so romantically through the latticed windows of the brand-new keep?

Although the Scottish Baronial was primarily a domestic style, it is interesting to note that it was also extensively employed for prisons.

A S the name implies, Second Empire Renaissance was a style that had its origins across the Channel, and while over here it never attained to its ripest development we can nevertheless boast sufficient examples to render it worthy of mention. Its most prominent feature, and that which unfortunately seems chiefly to have impressed those who sought to acclimatize it in England, was the mansard roof. However suitable this device may be on top of the Louvre it altogether fails to produce an effect of inevitable rightness amid the less exalted surroundings of Victoria Station. Unfortunately it had to recommend it the supreme quality of cheapness; with its aid a whole extra storey could be obtained at a considerable reduction of expense. As a result it has become the almost invariable termination for half the office blocks and luxury flats erected during the last half-century and at the moment its popularity shows few signs of diminution.

Other notable features of the style were the superabundance of shutters, whose purpose in nine cases out of ten was purely decorative, and at least one pair of ornamental urns suitable for the cultivation of the pinker varieties of geranium. The materials most favoured were yellow and red brick, pointed with great care and very white plaster, and Portland stone, elaborately rusticated, with every variety of slate and fancy leading for the roof. In England the style was generally employed for offices, hotels and railway stations, but one or two examples of its use in domestic architecture do nevertheless exist. They are, however, comparatively restrained in character and lack the staggering richness of such a masterpiece as the Travellers' Club in Paris.

THE peculiar danger inherent in all revivals is the inability to stop. Once a certain style has been revived there is, alas, no reason why one should not go ahead and revive all the others, and this is exactly the fate that overtook nineteenth-century architecture. Having reintroduced the Gothic with such success, the guardians of Victorian taste began seriously to consider whether there might not be some other historic style which had been hitherto overlooked that was more easily adapted to modern requirements than that of the ecclesiastical buildings of the thirteenth and fourteenth centuries. Towards the end of the third decade of the century there developed a suspicious enthusiasm for the architecture in vogue during the reign of a former dear Queen, and the streets of London were soon enlivened by the appearance of numerous buildings in a style that proudly proclaimed itself, on grounds that strike an unbiased observer as being exceedingly slender, as 'Queen Anne.'

The more remarkable features of this new style were a fondness for very bright red brick, a profusion of enrichments in that most deplorable of materials, terracotta, and a passion for breaking the skyline with every variety of gable that the genius of Holland had produced and a good many that it had not. Whole streets in the neighbourhood of Hans Place and Cadogan Gardens were re-erected in this new style and the cultured frequently pointed out, with considerable pride, that the wayfarer in that high-class residential district might easily imagine himself to be in Vermeer's Delft. As time went on, various other features, many of them borrowed from the Arts and Craft movement of the 'eighties, were incorporated in this style, of which perhaps the most important was a real loathing for symmetry that resulted in numberless bow windows bulging out in unexpected places and an inability to refrain from employing the most unsuitable materials, such as lead and beaten copper, in an unnecessary attempt to lend variety to an already hopelessly confused façade.

Inside, the decoration was even more striking. In all the principal rooms a low cornice, surmounting wallpaper that was either richly embossed in the Venetian manner or severely simple after Morris, jutted out into a wide shelf for the accommodation of blue china, while the fireplace was rendered cheerful by a surround of coloured tiles bearing a tasteful pattern of sunflowers by Walter Crane.

Fortunately many of the masterpieces of this style have survived untouched, and a short bus ride down Sloane Street will take the student to a district that has hardly changed since the day when Mr Wilde was called away from it on urgent business.

ART NOUVEAU

A T the end of the nineteenth century a certain malaise was discernible in the artistic world: which was not perhaps surprising, for after a prolonged surfeit of Municipal Gothic, Pont Street Dutch, Jubilee Renaissance and other exotic styles it is remarkable that the 'O-God-I'm-so-tired-of-it-all' attitude had not been adopted years before. However, until the late 'eighties William Morris, the celebrated inventor of the Simple Life, remained a voice calling in the willow-shrouded wilderness of Kelmscott. Now, however, his teaching bore a sudden crop of exceedingly odd fruit which in course of time came to be christened Art Nouveau.

While the hallmark of this new style was proudly claimed by its supporters to be extreme simplicity coupled with purity of line, honesty compels one to admit that, as one of its spiritual begetters said of truth, it was seldom pure and never simple. Asymmetry, which we noticed as being so popular in the later development of Pont Street Dutch, now became an absolute fetish. Walls staggered inwards from the base, gables shot up at the dizziest angles and doors and windows never by any chance appeared at the points where one was accustomed to find them. While it was originally conceived as a rural style, efforts were soon made to adapt it to urban requirements and rows of quaint and whimsey little cottages, all pebbledash and green shutters, appeared in the northern suburbs of London in clusters which their builders considered themselves justified (by the presence of two sunflowers and a box hedge) in calling Garden cities. Another interesting fact is that a row of such houses was never called a street but always a Way.

Rare and strange as was the aspect of the Art Nouveau house when seen from without, it was nevertheless the decoration of the interior which provided the exponents of the style with the opportunity for indulging in their finest flights of fancy. On a self-consciously austere mantelpiece, always three times too large for the grate and never less than five foot above the floor, reposed a couple of handmade earthenware pots of inconvenient shape and offensive green glaze, filled perhaps with a spray of cape gooseberries. While round the top of the wall ran a frieze of painted water lilies in a complicated and sinuous pattern that was repeated as likely as not in tiles or beaten copper over the fireplace.

From surroundings such as these did the New Woman emerge to bicycle off to an interesting meeting of the Fabian Society.

A S soon as the Boer War had been brought to satisfactory conclusion and the seventh Edward was safely seated on his throne, the country entered upon a brief but glittering Indian summer of prosperity and glory; and in order adequately to express the Imperial grandeurs of this epoch it was generally felt that some new and grandiose style of architecture was called for. It was soon decided that the style most suitable for the task of turning the capital of the British Empire into a bigger and better Potsdam was a modified form of Baroque.

Soon many of the principal streets of London were rendered ominous by the erection of numerous buildings of terrifying proportions and elephantine decoration. Beneath circular windows the size of the Round Pond (copied from Hampton Court, for it was thought proper to introduce a patriotic note here and there) vast swags of brobdingnagian fruit sprawled across the façade, threatening all beneath with instant annihilation should their security have been overestimated by the architect. In attitudes of acute discomfort nymphs and tribal deities of excessive female physique and alarming size balanced precariously on broken pediments, threatening the passer-by with a shower of stone fruit from the cavernous interiors of their inevitable cornucopia.

Alongside this neo-Baroque style in architecture there developed a characteristic form of Edwardian rococo in interior decoration which was not only decidedly less offensive but occasionally even achieved a certain tinselly but appropriate, if specious, charm, of which few examples have, alas, survived. Only the other day the exquisite plaster-work in the main Hall at Harrods was wantonly destroyed to make way for some tasteful modernistic improvements, but a few traces of decoration dating from this period are still visible in the baby linen department. Today almost the sole remaining masterpiece of the style is the restaurant and entrance hall of the Ritz Hotel.

DESPITE the international fame achieved by Art Nouveau its appeal had nevertheless been limited to a comparatively small coterie of Simple Lifers, Homespinners, Fabians, Suffragettes and the fifty-seven other fascinating varieties of British Intellectual. But as the new century advanced many of its features were introduced, not indeed in their original purity, to a far wider public. To meet the demands created by the rapid suburban development of London, more particularly in the south-western districts, a style was evolved which for lack of a better name we shall refer to as Wimbledon Transitional, which in its plentiful use of pebbledash, its giddy treatment of gables and its general air of self-conscious cosiness is plainly revealed as the unattractive offspring of Art Nouveau. Moreover, various other features of the style – for example, the fiendish variety of surface materials (frequently one finds pebbledash, ridge-tiling, fancy brickwork, weather-boarding and half-timbering all employed on the outside walls of the same building) – suggest that the other partner in the disgraceful liaison that gave it birth was none other than our old friend Pont Street Dutch.

However, it would be wrong to suppose that Wimbledon Transitional was a purely derivative style, for two of its most striking features had at the time an air of striking novelty. First, the skilful but unrestrained use of white painted wooden balconies, porches and verandas; second, the revival of half-timbering, a method of building which had been allowed to remain in a state of well-merited neglect for nearly three centuries. Thus Wimbledon Transitional occupies a position of peculiar importance in the history of modern British architecture, as being the connecting link between Pont Street Dutch and Art Nouveau, and such familiar modern styles as Stockbrokers' Tudor and Bypass Residential.

It is important to remember that at the time of its inception Wimbledon Transitional was essentially an upper-class style and attained its finest development in the £1,500–£2,000 a year districts of Surrey and the South Coast. It is still possible to find many splendid examples in these neighbourhoods that retain their original setting of conifers and rhododendrons and to see them at their best the serious student is advised to time his visit for sundown, when the pebbledash and the brickwork are bathed in a rich rosy glow and the Wellingtonias stand out black and menacing against the evening sky.

JUDGED by medieval standards of comfort the domestic buildings of the sixteenth century were doubtless almost luxurious; by any other criterion they had little to recommend them. The exigencies of timber construction kept the rooms low and cramped; the expense of glazing ensured that the windows would be few and small; and their claim to be considered beautiful can only be allowed on the grounds of sentiment or an undying attachment to the picturesque. Nevertheless, so deep and so widespread was the post-war devotion to the olde-worlde that an enormous number of such houses were erected, at considerable expense (for the methods of building general in Tudor times are nowadays as uneconomic as they are unnecessary), and the greatest ingenuity was displayed in providing the various modern devices with which they were anachronistically equipped with suitable olde-worlde disguises. Thus electrically produced heat warmed the hands of those who clustered enthusiastically round the yule logs blazing so prettily in the vast hearth; the light which shone so cosily from the old horn lantern was obtained from the grid; and from the depths of some old iron-bound chest were audible the dulcet tones of Mr Bing Crosby or the old-world strains of Mr Duke Ellington.

But worse was to come. At first, as noticed above, the expense had been considerable and prevented the adoption of the style by all but highclass builders working for wealthy clients, but soon the invention of new and cheaper methods of production brought it within the reach of the builders of Metroland. And today when the passer-by is a little unnerved at being suddenly confronted with a hundred and fifty accurate reproductions of Anne Hathaway's cottage, each complete with central heating and garage, he should pause to reflect on the extraordinary fact that all over the country the latest and most scientific methods of mass-production are being utilized to turn out a stream of old oak beams, leaded window panes and small discs of bottle-glass, all structural devices which our ancestors lost no time in abandoning as soon as an increase in wealth and knowledge enabled them to do so.

IN the troubled times in which we live it is perhaps not unnatural that many a longing glance should be cast at those periods of the past of which we like to persuade ourselves a profound tranquillity was the keynote. Nor is it surprising that no class of the community should have been so deeply affected by this form of nostalgia as the bankers, although it must be admitted that the period of their choice, the eighteenth century, bore in actual fact little or no resemblance to the roast-beef and Reynolds, gilt-edged and candle-lit world of their dreams. However, solidity was the quality they sought and solidity was the quality with which they retrospectively endowed the age of the French Revolution. It was not the first time that wish fulfilment has operated in the formation of an architectural style.

The architects who were favoured had, as a rule, rather less understanding of the nature and practice of eighteenth-century architecture than the bankers who employed them, and the resulting style, known as Bankers' Georgian, always preserves something of the air of a Metro-Goldwyn-Mayer production of the *School for Scandal*; a certain restlessness arising from the knowledge that no expense is to be spared, but at the same time refinement must remain the watchword. Moreover, owing possibly to the fact that one of the masters of the style hails from the outposts of Empire, a curious provincialism is frequently discernible, particularly in the treatment of detail which, while it brings a bracing whiff of the veldt into the stuffy atmosphere of Lombard Street, does little to preserve the illusion of the eighteenth century.

At the moment Bankers' Georgian is still one of the most popular of our modern styles and hundreds of examples are visible in London and the provinces. Apart from a suspicious newness and a superabundance of plate glass, the almost invariable feature by which it can easily be distinguished from the genuine article is the high-pitched bogus-mansard roof. It should not, however, be confused with the two related but yet distinct styles, Office of Works Queen Anne and Architectural Association (or *Beggars' Opera*) Georgian. The latter may readily be distinguished by its invincible refinement while the former always preserves an unmistakable air of having just been run-up by the little woman round the corner.

THIS style, which attained great popularity both in this country and in America (where it was generally known as Spanish-colonial), is actually our old friend Pont Street Dutch with a few Stockholm trimmings and a more daring use of colour. In the most typical examples the walls are whitewashed, the roof is covered with Roman tiles in a peculiarly vehement shade of green, and the windows have been enriched with a great deal of fancy leading of a tortuous ingenuity. It was the upper-class style *par excellence* of the pre-slump years, but latterly has sunk a little in the social scale and occasional examples are now to be found alongside some of our more exclusive bypasses.

Within, the decoration was almost always carried out in Curzon Street ecclesiastical-Spanish with a plentiful supply of Knole sofas, large Baroque candlesticks fitted with lampshades made out of old sheets of music or maps, and an occasional wrought-iron grill. The walls were usually stippled in peach or sea-green shades and sometimes ingenious tricks of shading were employed. It provided the invariable background against which the characters in Messrs Lonsdale's and Coward's earlier plays cracked their epigrams and its presence may always be assumed in the novels of Mr Arlen.

While it was essentially a country-house style and many of its greatest masterpieces are located on the sea-coast, a few examples are to be found in the more expensive suburbs of the capital and it can be studied in all its diversity in the neighbourhood of Hampstead.

IF an architect of enormous energy, painstaking ingenuity and great structural knowledge, had devoted years of his life to the study of the problem of how best to achieve the maximum of inconvenience, in the shape and arrangement under one roof of a stated number of rooms, and had had the assistance of a corps of research workers ransacking architectural history for the least attractive materials and building devices known in the past, it is just possible, although highly unlikely, that he might have evolved a style as crazy as that with which the speculative builder, at no expenditure of mental energy at all, has enriched the landscape on either side of our great arterial roads. As one passes by one can amuse one's self by classifying the various contributions which past styles have made to this infernal amalgam; here are some quaint gables culled from Art Nouveau surmounting a façade that is plainly Modernistic in inspiration; there the twisted beams and leaded panes of Stockbrokers' Tudor are happily contrasted with bright green tiles of obviously Pseudish origin; next door some terracotta plaques, Pont Street Dutch in character, enliven a white wood Wimbledon Transitional porch, making it a splendid foil to a red-brick garage that is vaguely Romanesque in feeling. But while he is heavily indebted to history for the majority of his decorative and structural details (in almost every case the worst features of the style from which they were filched), in the planning and disposition of his erections the speculative builder displays a genius that is all his own. Notice the skill with which the houses are disposed, that ensures that the largest possible area of countryside is ruined with the minimum of expense; see how carefully each householder is provided with a clear view into the most private offices of his next-door neighbour and with what studied disregard of the sun's aspect the principal rooms are planned.

It is sad to reflect that so much ingenuity should have been wasted on streets and estates which will inevitably become the slums of the future. That is, if a fearful and more sudden fate does not obliterate them prematurely; an eventuality that does much to reconcile one to the prospect of aerial bombardment.

N O architectural development of our time has done so much to change the face of our cities and indirectly to alter the whole tempo of our social life as the coming of the large block of luxury flats. As a means of housing a large number of people in a crowded urban area it has much to recommend it, but unfortunately, owing to a variety of causes, it has been accorded a hearty welcome at the wrong end of the social scale. As a result, those residential districts such as Mayfair, which are of the greatest interest architecturally, have been ruthlessly cut up in order to make way for truncated red-brick tenement buildings, which may quite possibly with the addition of another thirty storeys achieve a certain monumental impressiveness in the neighbourhood of Park Avenue, but which are completely unsuited to Park Lane; while the inhabitants of other districts which should long ago have been demolished are forced, if they wish to move, to trek out to the scabrous housing estates that are rapidly devouring what remains of the open spaces in the home counties.

The most extraordinary feature of the whole business, however, remains the fantastic illogicality which prompts those who could well afford comfortable and dignified homes to live in a collection of centrally-heated matchboxes in a building resembling a pickle factory inconsequently decorated with a few stage props left over from a provincial production of *The Beggars' Opera*, carefully situated at the noisiest corner of the busiest available thoroughfare, and at a rental three times the cost of running all but the most grandiose town house.

THE all too few blocks of working-class flats, although similar in many respects to the Park Lane variety, are nevertheless easily distinguishable by reason of a number of interesting features. First, they are always situated in a much quieter neighbourhood; secondly, the rents are much lower though the rooms are seldom any smaller; thirdly, they are usually rather better architecturally. True, they too look like pickle factories, but quite good pickle factories; not, it must be admitted, owing to any particular skill on the part of the architect, but solely to the fact that there has not been sufficient money to waste on Portland stone facings and other decorative trimmings. The convenience of the tenants is a consideration that is invariably treated with the same lordly disregard in both varieties.

If, however, you are still in doubt as to which category any particular block of flats belongs (for occasionally it so happens that the builders of Park Lane blocks are at a loss to find a really noisy site and local authorities are sometimes in a position to push up the rates and so afford a few decorative urns and a lot of fancy tiling) it is advisable to see what name is inscribed over the entrance; in nine cases out of ten, if it has 'buildings' tacked on it is a working-class block, whereas if it has 'house' it comes under the luxury heading. If all else fails, see if there are any trees in the immediate neighbourhood; if there are, it may undoubtedly be classified as L.C.C., as there is nothing which the luxury flat architect hates so much as a tree, and not only will he take great care not to plant any but will go to infinite trouble to ensure the destruction of any that may already be there.

WHEN, shortly after the War, the Modern Movement (q.v.) was first brought to the public notice it led to a natural and healthy reaction against the excessive ornament with which the architects of the previous generation had so abundantly enriched their façades; but unfortunately a great number of architects and builders, being completely out of sympathy with the ideals of the true supporters of the movement, wasted no time in happily turning this novel simplicity to their own ends. The great advantage, in their eyes, of these large expanses of plain wall free from the burden of heavy cornices, swags of fruit and elaborate rustication, lay in the splendid surface they presented for the application of a whole new series of ornaments, more cheery in appearance and more expressive of the tastes of the age of jazz. Thus the buildings which cultured and disinterested men had at length succeeded in freeing from the burden of out-worn academic impedimenta were now enlivened by the addition of quite meaningless scrolls and whirls in a fiendish variety of materials, ranging from chromium plate to bakelite, which the ingenuity of modern science had placed at the disposal of every tuppenny-hapenny builder in the country. So the last state of British architecture was even worse than the first, for the earlier forms of applied decoration, hideous, misused and unnecessary as they had become, had at least some thin, tenuous connection with a once vital tradition, whereas these bars of beaten copper, these sheets of black glass, these friezes of chromium pomegranates, not only did not arise out of the demands of construction but had not the slightest shred of tradition to provide a threadbare excuse for their revolting existence.

Numerous examples of the Modernistic are to be found in all our principal cities, and such of our great luxury cinemas as are not built in Metro-Goldwyn Renaissance are almost without exception conspicuous masterpieces of this style. Incidentally, the Modernistic is not confined exclusively to architecture, but has made itself felt in the realm of interior decoration and has had a peculiarly disastrous effect on typography.

'THE history of civilization . . . leaves in architecture its truest, because its most unconscious, record.'

However, the late Mr Geoffrey Scott when he wrote those words had not had the inestimable privilege of observing, in Herr Hitler, the Architect as Man of Action. So that while the main contention expressed in the above sentence remains unassailable, the subsidiary clause may be thought to stand in need of some slight modification. After all those speeches about building for the future, for generations of pure-bred Aryans yet unborn, can we still subscribe to the view that the record is always unconscious? These gigantic pillars, these megalithic colonnades, this so obvious austerity, are they not designed with one eye on the future? With the fully conscious hope that posterity will say 'Here was a race of supermen, the builders of a civilization that was moved by a stern and splendid purpose and buttressed by an unbelievable solidity'? Surely the modern German architecture is in the nature of a reinsurance clause that will compensate the noble Teuton for the crass stupidity which prevents his contemporaries from appreciating the nobility, firmness and idealism of his present regime, by making certain of the admiration of the future.

For, alas, the non-German has not been overwhelmed with admiration. He realizes, unless blinded by ideology, that some of these buildings are not without merit – they frequently achieve a definite if rather empty dignity and there is welcome freedom from fussy ornament – but he remembers that the whole thing has already been done a great deal better. Napoleon too had his creative whims and as an architectural expression of 'sacro egoismo' the first Empire style, as developed in the layout and planning of Paris, makes the masterpieces of our latter-day dictators look empty, bombastic and ridiculous. It was, indeed, unfortunate for Herr Hitler that the German pavilion at the Paris exhibition should have been within a hundred miles of the Arc de Triomphe.

WHEN a New Age dawned and the Soviet state was born, we were all told by its many admirers that now we should see what the proletarian architect could accomplish when freed from the shackles of capitalistic patronage. This new freedom, it could not be doubted, would accomplish that for which architectural reformers had been striving for years, a new and vital architecture cleanly expressive of its purpose and unencumbered with all those fripperies which the degraded taste of an outworn civilization had clung to as symbols of bourgeois taste and importance. It was therefore all the more distressing, that after a long period of waiting the architecture which finally emerged should have been so difficult to distinguish from that produced by the less inspired academic architects working as wage slaves of capitalism. But sad as was this disappointment, it was still more depressing when it was discovered that the minor details wherein it differed from the architecture of effete social-democracy were just those which strike an unbiased observer as being most reminiscent of the architecture of international fascism. The same emphasis on size, the same tendency to imagine that beauty is to be achieved by merely abolishing ornament, regardless of the fact that it is dependent on the proportions of what is then revealed, the same declamatory and didactic idiom. There exist, of course, one or two very minor differences, such as the Soviet architect's habit of eschewing the use of the capital on ideological grounds; but in essentials the two styles remain the same. And when, as happened in Paris last year, they are brought face to face, it is immediately apparent that the proletarian and the Fascist both labour under the same misapprehension – that political rhetoric is a sufficient substitute for genuine architectural inspiration.

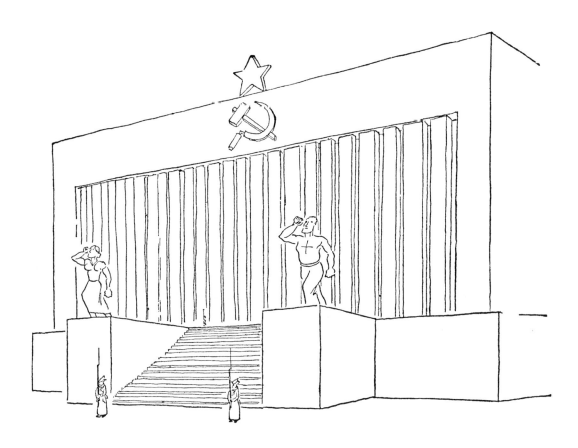

SHORTLY before the War a number of accomplished, disinterested and original architects came to the sad conclusion that architecture had died somewhere about the end of the first quarter of the nineteenth century and that therefore it was no longer any use continuing hopeless efforts at revival but that a completely new start must be made. Modern life, they argued, was governed by mechanical principles, and therefore the rules which held good for the construction of machines must now be applied to architecture. That this doctrine rests on a fallacy need not blind us to the fact that in practice it produced buildings of considerable merit and had a most excellent and revivifying effect on modern architecture. It led to a ruthless abandonment of all ornamentation, and although the example of the eighteenth century and antiquity are sufficient to disprove the belief that decoration is in itself deplorable, no ornaments are undoubtedly preferable to bad ones. Thus the style which now emerged was one of the utmost austerity, relying for its effect on planning and proportion alone, and faithfully fulfilling the one condition to which every importance was attached, of 'fitness for purpose.' Admirable as were the results in the case of factories, airports, hospitals and other utilitarian buildings, when the same principle was applied to domestic architecture, the success was not always so marked. For one thing, the new architects could seldom resist making a house fit for purposes such as sunbathing, which the English climate and environment frequently rendered impossible of fulfilment; for another, the conception of a house as 'une machine à habiter' presupposes a barrenness of spirit to which, despite every indication of its ultimate achievement, we have not yet quite attained.

However, it remains a style of which any thoughtless disparagement is to be heartily deplored; let us withhold our criticism and regard it as a means rather than an end. Once we have ceased thinking of it as completely developed style in itself, its minor faults – that passion for pavement lights, that tendency to cantilever for the sake of cantilevering – become of small importance. For just as the cubist movement in painting produced little of any permanent artistic worth but nevertheless provided a most valuable discipline for a number of painters, so it is to be hoped that from this bare functional style will one day emerge a genuine modern architecture that need fear no comparison with the great styles of the past.

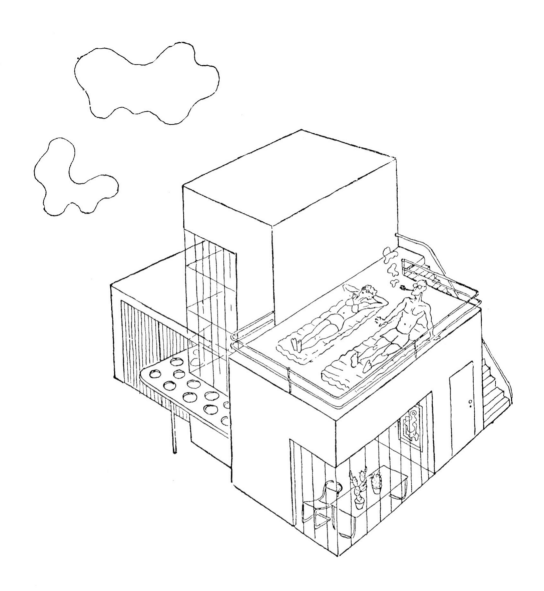